letters to dead artists

faridah cameron

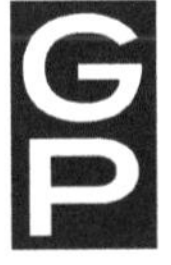

Letters to Dead Artists
ISBN 978-1-76109-927-4

Cover image: Faridah Cameron
Cover Design and typesetting: Rack and Rune
First published 2025 by
GINNINDERRA PRESS
PO Box 2 Bentleigh 3204
ginninderrapress.com.au

Acknowledgements

The first of these letters was written in response to a prompt in a writing workshop for visual artists run by Ruth Hadlow. Thank you Ruth for the prompt, and for reminding me that writing as well as painting is a joyful and rewarding thing to do.

I spend most of my life in the studio. Thank you to my dear family for their endless support and understanding, especially my partner in all things, Neil Cameron.

And thank you to Deb and Mandy and in the first instance Stephen at Ginninderra Press for keeping the banner for the arts and creativity flying high.

Contents

Introduction

These letters are not art critique. The artists to whom they are addressed have all produced work that has caused me to think new thoughts, given me pause, moved me in mysterious ways. The letters are my unguarded response.

We humans have been making images and responding to them for millennia. There is no right or wrong way to respond to a piece of art. What you think, what you feel, reflects what life has taught you so far. Whether or not you like what you're seeing, if a work of art speaks to you at all it's worth your while to listen. It can tell you more about the world in which we live and it can also tell you a lot about yourself.

To Agnes Martin

7 August 2019

My Dear Agnes,

You were already nearly gone by the time I heard of you, already painting the looming black shapes that preceded your death. I recognised in them something of importance to me, although I could not have said what. And then you were gone.

Nevertheless, having seen *White Flower* at the Guggenheim and having read whatever I could find about you and your work in the meantime, twelve years later I came looking for you – an adventure embarked upon in a clapped-out, bullet-holed truck driven by a recovering alcoholic who looked alarmingly like Vincent Van Gogh in a cowboy hat. Ken had been a friend and colleague of my husband Neil's many years earlier. A talented mural painter in his younger days, by now Ken's paintings and sculptures overflowed his home and its grounds, his shed, a bus, the roadside and so on, and his art could best be described as 'raw'. He harboured a deep resentment of anyone who had ever enjoyed any success in the arts; and I'm afraid that although he had never seen your work, Agnes, and knew you only by reputation, that included you.

He recognised however that it was important to me so, in an act of true friendship, he took us from his home in Madrid, New Mexico, on the two-hour drive to Taos, the town closest to the place where you spent so many years of your life.

Taos, I had read, was where the Harwood Museum of Art was to be found, and the Harwood contained the largest group of your paintings on display anywhere. Why, I wondered, were your paintings available only sporadically in the major centres, when your work was so wonderful? Do people have such short memories? Or is this some logical concomitant of your reclusiveness during life?

In Taos, no one seemed to know where the Harwood was located. I had the address, but the street with that name leading off the main square was little more than a walkway. About thirty yards from the museum's entrance a rather bleary young couple enjoying lunchtime sangrias on their veranda said they had never heard of it.

We found it, but it was not the imposing edifice I had imagined. We made our way through the rooms of what had been a large private home: Room 1, El Tatuaje: The Tattoo in Underground Culture; Room 5, Lowbrow Insurgence: the Rise of Post-Pop Art, and so on. And there, at the back of the first floor we found the Agnes Martin Gallery, a room specially built to house your seven magnificent paintings.

I don't need to tell you that I loved them, certainly don't need to describe to you of all people their shimmering presence, their stunning luminosity, which no reproduction could possibly capture.

The reason I'm writing this is in fact to thank you, for bringing your art into the world and for the example of your life as an artist. For having the courage, I suppose, to speak of perfection, to which you say your work aspired, but which you never expected it to achieve. For your idealism, which I still believe has a place in the world, and for the optimism implicit in your paintings and in the titles you gave them. If you will forgive my presumption: for the dignity with which you managed the difficulties your life presented. For what I perceive to be your dedication and your integrity.

I wished I had had the chance to tell you this in person, but in your absence I found myself talking about you with the woman at the front desk. That is how I learnt that you had asked to be buried here at the Harwood, near the paintings you had so generously donated; and that permission had been refused; and that people who loved you had climbed the fence at night and placed your ashes under the peach tree, marked only by a small circular cement paver. So at least I was able to visit that, and to say goodbye.

On the way back to Madrid, the full moon rose over the mountains in the direction of your home and something about the light of it across that vast plain entered my being. I don't think I'm being fanciful – I'm sure you know what I mean. Some memories and the feelings that attend them remain vital long after the event.

I send to you my deepest respect and, again, my thanks for having so profoundly enriched my life.

I do not, of course, expect a reply.

With fondest regards,
Faridah Cameron

PS: Ken loved the paintings.

To Barnett Newman

27 November 2020

Dear Mr Newman

It may seem a little late in the day for me to be writing to you. I first discovered your 'zip' paintings and fell in love with them when I was at art school more than thirty years ago; however, to be frank, I haven't thought about them very often since. Consequently, before attempting to write to you, I looked you up on the internet to reacquaint myself with some particulars of your life and work.

You were Jewish, married, and dwelt in New York. It seems that you lived largely off your wife's teaching salary until quite late, when your paintings finally began to sell. I wondered how an apparently quite conservative fellow like yourself (love the moustache, by the way) might accept that situation. The answer is perhaps to be found in your writings. You spoke of the 'seemingly insane drive of man to be a painter' and concluded that it was 'an act of defiance against man's fall and an assertion that he return to the Garden of Eden', the Garden of Eden being presumably the antidote to your 'struggle against bourgeois society' and 'total rejection of it'.

Apart from the overt religious references (I daresay you came from a family that took its Jewishness seriously, and could never find a way to abandon your early learnings entirely) and the term 'man' to imply the whole of the human race (which I shall allow as a generational blip), I find that I am strongly in sympathy with your views. I too suffer from the insane drive and have largely abandoned bourgeois values. (Perhaps perforce. It's hard to maintain a bourgeois lifestyle on an artist's earnings.) I too had a religious education, but I live now in what is called 'a secular age' and have access to many other streams of thought, both philosophical and scientific, than were available in the mid-twentieth century, so it has been much easier to sort it all out. But the values we were taught as children are what we fall back on in order to accommodate the 'insane drive': they form the infrastructure upon which to build the practice of an innate spirituality within a materially sparse lifestyle.

So I suppose it was the innate spirituality in your work to which I responded all those years ago at art school in Darwin, although I doubt I could have articulated it then. As a New Yorke,r you'd have hated Darwin, I'm sure, but I think you might have appreciated the Indigenous art that exists there, the particular forms of abstraction. Would Rothko have liked them too, I wonder? His work was so much about diffusion, like walking through a door and feeling oneself dissolve, while yours was more like seeing light coming through the crack of a door at the other side of a dark room. In Aboriginal paintings, there are no doors. And there's no emptiness. They don't imply a 'somewhere else': everything is entirely integrated. Their canvases are joyous, filled and fulfilled. That's how I see them anyway. They speak of spirituality of a different kind: a life lived rather than pursued.

The question arises: why am I writing to you now? I've just started a new painting. Its main feature is a narrow strip of seaweed running straight down the middle. When I saw what I had done I was strongly reminded of your zips. So I thought

I'd write and let you know, and acknowledge the connection. I'm sure my painting echoes something I gained from your own work – another example of early influence finding its way into the here and now – and I thank you for it.

I did see your Stations of the Cross at the Miho Museum of Art in Japan a couple of years ago. I wondered why you had taken on that particular story. Surprisingly, I found the paintings disappointing. I mean no disrespect. There were marks that I can only imagine were stains from masking tape you used during their construction. (I made a cautionary note about the use of masking tape.) However, I'd love to see them again in more sympathetic lighting and after a good clean. I imagine you would have been disappointed too, so I'm sorry now to have mentioned it. However, I thought you would like to know that your work is still greatly appreciated internationally, especially (according to Wikipedia) as a fine influence on later painters. Even in this secular age. And certainly by me.

I trust this finds you in some painterly Eden no longer driven by earthly insanity, if in some part of yourself you retained some hope of that. Wouldn't it be lovely if after death we all achieved the precise paradise we crave? (A discussion I hope to take up in my correspondence with Fra Angelico.)

With sincere good wishes
Faridah Cameron

To Francis Bacon

28 November 2020

Dear Francis

I hardly know how to begin. Your life and mine have been lived so differently that I'm surprised we share a language. In painterly terms, I'm not sure that we do. Despite my aim to think outside the box (pun unintended but accepted) my paintings, it must be admitted, reveal a deep engagement with all things traditionally associated with womanhood, and a certain idealism. I was a good girl: you were a bad boy.

It seems your behaviour was generally risky if not reprehensible (who am I to judge?) And I think you paid for it. Your best known paintings are sometimes harshly lit interrogations and sometimes shrieks of pain. Strangely, I love them for that: for their uncompromising account of a life experience so far from my own, in paintings that still somehow manage to remain guileless. They are filled with masterful aesthetic tricks but they never present as arch or insincere. Which is odd, because I suspect that in life you were capable of being very arch, and most likely insincere.

I've seen Figures at the Base of the Cross and so on in the Tate Modern, but it's not really those that I want to write to you about. It's the portraits. I saw quite a large collection of them at the Art Gallery of New South Wales years ago and they have stayed with me so strongly. It's partly the way you have applied the paint: the sureness of the stroke, the swift the pull of the brush (or was it a sponge?), the actual size of whatever you've used to apply opaque pigments in a single stroke broken by the texture of the paint beneath. I have heard these works described as distorted, but I don't see them that way. Instead, the effect is one of movement, of passing from one position to another. Often, they seem to record the moment at which someone carefully observed suddenly turns their head to return the gaze of the onlooker. So passing from one position to another not just in terms of pose but also in terms of relationship to the artist. It's that moment of recognition just before whatever will happen proceeds, the moment of potential interaction. It's the look you exchange with a new lover when you're engaged in a conversation with someone else, or an old lover when something is about to be said after a long silence. In that sense, I find them quite romantic. There is longing in them. And sometimes they are the moment of disengagement. Disregard. Even disdain. But so instantaneous – so evocative.

So many docos have been made about you, Francis. The one in the pub with Melvyn Bragg was undoubtedly the best, when you spoke for yourself. I saw one just the other night; some of your friends were interviewed, but also the curators who seemed to think they knew what you thought. Such impertinence. But in the end, it's just the paintings that matter and, Francis, they do matter to me. I'm sorry if your life was a rough trot. From my position, it certainly looks as if it was. But I turn, Francis, in an act that may seem to be a distortion of the position I usually hold, I look towards you, and I see your beauty.

Faridah

To Frida Kahlo

10 December 2020

Dear Frida,

Although I am an artist, my letter to you is not so much about art as about human behaviour, human proclivities.

A little history: in the late 1980s, I was working on community arts projects with young women not long out of drama school. They were quite enamoured of you and, although they seemed not to have paid your paintings much serious attention, your personal appearance and your reportedly adventurous sexual conduct made you something of a feminist icon for them. (Although you may not be acquainted with the feminist ideals of the time, I feel you would have greeted them with enthusiasm.)

Your name has remained widely known – uniquely, I think, among women artists of your time, except perhaps for Georgia O'Keefe. However, in recent years, visiting Mexico during the Day of the Dead, I came across you in a quite different context. There was your portrait, reverentially placed among the sugar skulls and marigolds on many home altars. It appeared that in Mexico you had now become revered in an almost religious way. How might one account for this?

It is well documented that your physical injury caused you great suffering, which you bore throughout your life with stoicism and grace. Mexico, with its gilded churches, banks of lit candles, votive offerings, is actively a Catholic country. There are obvious parallels between your life and those of the saints; however, I'm sure you would agree that other aspects of your character would be unlikely to fit the mould. You advocated for the culture of your homeland and its people, so you might be seen as a hero of nationalism; yet I saw not one altar image of your husband Diego, whose wonderful murals still stand testament to your shared dedication to this cause.

We visited your home, the Blue House, and thought it very beautiful. I could easily imagine myself living in such a space. However, I was dismayed to see on display so much evidence of your pain: the false leg that you carefully concealed under your long skirts; the stained wheelchair. It's true that I was unwell myself that day after a bad flight, but I found the pathos and, frankly, the indignity of these objects overwhelming and had to retreat to the garden to recover.

It was as if your suffering, not your work, was the central subject. We were able to find very few of your paintings in the house or anywhere in Mexico. Most of them were overseas on tour, so be assured that your work does live on worldwide. I caught up with some of it later, in Sydney. Two lively young women were standing in front of one of your portraits, photographing themselves with a false moustache stuck over their eyebrows. They were enjoying themselves, being rather frivolous, but they were also declaring an allegiance with you.

I think the gift of your paintings is the directness with which they tell your story. They are a statement, not a plea. You look straight at us. Your self-portraiture openly depicts your pain but never seems to require anything more of the viewer than to be seen. You display your strength, but do not ask for sympathy. Perhaps your uncompromising self-possession is the quality you bring to young women in the more affluent countries today.

It occurs to me only now, as I write, that the ceremonies involved with the Day of the Dead are more ancient than those of the Church. These altars are not in fact intended for religious worship, but to invite the return of the spirit. Perhaps the Mexican people invite your spirit back because in today's world they need your courage and strength. It's possible too that this is one of the many pre-Christian practices that the Church as adapted for its own purposes – they call it sainthood and intercession.

To be frank, and I'm glad I do not have to say this to you in person, I have never felt that your paintings were particularly good. Your popularity is not about the paintings, it's about your personality. This much I knew. But I see it now, Frida. How clever of you. Unwittingly or otherwise, you have painted your own icons.

You have my admiration.

Your sister in art,
Faridah

To Maria Sibylla Merian

16 January 2021

Dear Ms Merian

This letter comes to you from far away in time and space and yet I feel we have much in common.

I was never able to realise my ambition to study entomology, but I have retained a great love of the natural world which I am sure infuses my art. I too am fascinated by insects. It is easy to understand that a human baby once it enters the world simply grows, but that a grub should encapsulate itself and then emerge later as a butterfly never ceases to amaze me and I gather you were one of the very first people to understand and, in your paintings, document this phenomenon.

In their adult form, insects have a special appeal not only because of their extraordinary colours and markings but also their delicacy of form. How is it possible that the tiny legs of a flea enable it to jump such a distance? How does a moth detect the wing beat of a potential mate kilometres away? Despite the invention of the internet, I have still not managed to learn the answer to these questions and I daresay that you, as the keenest observer of all that crawls and flies but having lived at the very outset of the Age of Science, don't know either.

In the early years of this century – around 2007, I think – a selection of nature drawings and paintings was chosen from the British Royal Collection and assembled as an exhibition entitled

Amazing Rare Things – a description taken, I gather, from a remark of your own. David Attenborough had a hand in it. (You won't know him, which is rather a pity; he expresses huge respect for you and I'm sure the feeling would have been mutual.)

I came across the exhibition by accident. We had been visiting the recently completed Scottish Houses of Parliament, an expensive architectural abomination close to the Queen's Edinburgh residence, Holyrood House. After leaving the parliament buildings in a state of some despair at the capacity of human beings to, with the best of intentions, get things so horribly wrong, we noticed the Queen's Gallery across the road.

The building itself was architecturally mellow, the unpretentious modern internal fittings having been chosen to blend cleverly with the historic framework. This in itself restored our spirits somewhat; but the exhibition housed within was simply a joy. It included drawings by Leonardo; yet even in that august company, your work was outstanding.

Your paintings had a luminescence that few artists have managed to achieve before or since. Such vitality! Such presence! This could only have come from observing the living creatures directly and studying their ways. I was in awe, not only of your obvious dedication to task and your very skilful painting but also of the sense of wonderment and delight in these extraordinary little beings that your work so clearly conveyed.

My favourite paintings were the ones you did during your time in Suriname (notwithstanding the fact that I could hardly look at the tarantulas, so real were they). Mind you, I note that you had scant regard for scale, and you did tend to add incongruous elements for artistic effect. Although this might not have withstood scientific scrutiny, it gave a context and lent a sense of drama, creatively implying a narrative.

Leonardo's extraordinary drawings from nature are a scientific exploration, a fervid attempt to understand. He strives for accuracy. That the drawings also qualify as art is, in his hands, inevitable. You, however, lent your imagination to your work in a way that has no equivalent in the scientific illustrations of your own time or since. In the world of Fine Art that I inhabit, 'representation' and 'illustration' have become rather derogatory terms. However, there is no doubt in my mind that your work transcends any such labels. As Picasso once said, 'Art is the lie that reveals the truth.' (I doubt you'd have liked his paintings but he certainly understood his business.)

You were in Suriname from 1699 to 1701, during the Age of Discovery, which soon became the Age of Science. Now we are immersed in the Technological Age. G.K. Chesterton was once quoted as saying, 'Where is the wisdom we lost in knowledge? Where is the knowledge we lost in information?' Even though we now have access to knowledge and information as never before, current wisdom undoubtedly involves the understanding that we humans are an integral part of the natural world, not superior to it, despite our longstanding belief that it is our right to exploit other life forms and the earth itself for our own benefit.

In fact, we know now that the future of the human race depends upon our ability to modify our behaviour. Perhaps a key to this lies in regaining our sense of wonder. Your beautiful paintings, which reawaken the joy of discovery, can surely help us to do that. ('Beautiful' is also considered something of a dirty word in the arts, by the way, which I am afraid indicates how far we have strayed from a simply harmonious existence…)

In Edinburgh, your paintings provided a soothing antidote to human inaptitude and ugliness. In the world today, foolishness is rife. Your work, by contrast, stands as an assertion of the joy to be gained from an appreciation of the natural world, and an affirmation of the value of art.

For this, my deepest thanks.

Respectfully,
Faridah Cameron

To Clarice Beckett

17 June 2021

Dear Clarice

My friends and I are staying on Bruny Island, off the coast of Tasmania, engaged in something of a field trip. Our field trips are informal things, really a coming together of friends who share common interests, but they do result in writings and photographic journals and sculptural and photographic assemblage and, in my case, paintings.

Last night during those hours of waking that seem unavoidable these days, I studied the catalogue of your recent show at the Art Gallery of South Australia. The catalogue is a very handsome publication. It seems that the powers that be have decided to put you back on the map.

It must have been very difficult to have your work dismissed by the arts establishment as it generally was during your lifetime. I hope you will take heart in the knowledge that the views of your critics, now quoted, read as arrogant and inappropriate. I don't think such harsh judgements could be published these days. I've no doubt the critics are just as opinionated, but by now they've learned to leave themselves more room to manoeuvre. However, the catalogue writer praised you effusively.

We have not had good weather since arriving here yesterday. This morning it rained continuously so we set out to drive to the lighthouse at the southern tip of the island. I'm afraid I was feeling rather despondent as we made our way up and down the steep path and negotiated the muddy approach to the rather dismal little museum. As we turned to drive home, however, one of my friends asked to take a detour to Jetty Beach.

The rain had paused and the air was very still. We made our way through tall eucalypts down to the crescent of a protected bay where clear, waveless water lapped gently. A group of gulls floated not far away. We walked slowly, as we usually do, the length of the beach, between thick drifts of kelp, finding ruffles of delicate lacelike coral, blue-green crab pincers, fluorescent pink seaweed, seaweed like Chinese noodles. I was slightly ahead of my friends as I reached the end of the beach where I was met by a pair of oystercatchers who seemed to accept my presence without fear. As I watched them, admiring their red eyes, red legs and long red beaks against the dark grey of the rocks, the sun suddenly broke through and I stood for some minutes, bathed in warmth. It was a lovely experience.

As we set off for home, the rain began again. The lowering light through misty rain, reflected hazily on the water of the bay, reminded us of your paintings.

We were reminded of your paintings, even though the atmosphere of this place is so very different from the Melbourne that you knew. I grew up in Melbourne, in those bayside suburbs. I remember sunburnt days on Brighton beach, bathing boxes at Anglesea, exploring the rocks at Ricketts Point. My cousins lived in Sandringham. Not long ago, I scattered a dear friend's ashes at Beaumaris Beach, near her father's old house. I vividly remember the colour of evening light, headlamps reflected on wet roads after dark, and the relative emptiness of the streets.

Yours is the Melbourne I remember from childhood, even though I lived there twenty years after your death. You caught the mood so well. Now the streets are crowded with cars. People do not walk silhouetted down streets wattle-lined and unkerbed. The mood has changed. Like the jetty on Jetty Beach, only remnants remain.

After walking on Jetty Beach my thoughts were these.

Although your paintings open into a fulsome and airy space, their high horizon line tends to lend an easy intimacy of approach. Even looking across ocean or into sky, one feels grounded, as if taking a walk. While the arrangement within the picture frame is careful and deliberate, I imagine you instinctively recognised the potential in the scene and painted it just as you came upon it. Your images have swiftly captured evanescent personal impressions of the world around you.

My own paintings are very different. They are drawn from within myself, an amalgam of impressions gained over a lifetime. They refer to natural phenomena, but seen through the lens of memory. Their aspect is entirely flat, without perspective, like a piece of cloth. They are created slowly over many months, not quickly as a response to an immediate reality.

In this, we are opposites, and yet I feel a kinship with your work.

I think both your paintings and mine are essentially female in nature. Within 'the landscape', you evoke an intimacy of experience unconcerned with the grand vista. The people in your paintings are where women instinctively rest their eyes – the distance at which children can be seen playing. My work is at the length of an arm, an expression of things seen and noted previously, worked out in the domestic context of making and mending.

Your marks are soft and indistinct, mine are as uncompromising as the line of stitch that they resemble, and yet I think both (and I hope I am not flattering myself here) trigger memories and associations and therefore resonate effectively.

There is a delicacy in your work, Clarice, that mine entirely lacks, and yet both reveal distinct sensibilities which are not incompatible. Your paintings were numbered in the thousands; if I work consistently for the next twenty years, I might only achieve a couple of hundred, and yet by that time I will have lived and painted for some forty years longer than you. At this point in time, my work receives little notice. I would like to hope that one day it might be seen to have some lasting worth, as is the case for yours now.

Currently, the collectors, curators and gallerists are congratulating themselves on their achievements in bringing your work to popular attention and lasting acclaim. However, I would like to reserve my congratulations for you, Clarice, without whom the arts scene would have nothing to crow about. Congratulations on having held your ground, painted what was meaningful to you and produced a fine body of work without the support and approval of the arts nabobs.

It seems your time has come rather too late for you to enjoy it. I imagine that many artists like myself will wonder whether that would have mattered to you. On behalf of us all, I send greetings to you in the beyond.

Yours sincerely,
Faridah

To Fra Angelico

2 November 2021

My Dear Fra Angelico,

In writing to you, it would please me very much to imagine that you now reside in the heaven that you depicted in your paintings. You dedicated your life to Christianity, so it would seem only fair for you to be granted the appropriate reward. Wouldn't it be wonderful if we all managed to attain after death whatever state it is that we desire?

The world has changed so much since your death in 1455. However, I wish to address matters of the spirit and I do not imagine that the human spirit is much altered since your time, despite the evolution of ideas.

Some years ago in London, I saw a section of your San Marco altarpiece. I was amazed at the character evident in the faces of patrons, friars and saints and in their poses – at the finesse of your brushwork, the subtlety and vibrancy of colour, the delicacy of the detail. The skin tones, the haloes… I was, and I remain, full of admiration. Importantly, your work represents, I think, the purest vision of what Christianity (at least the Roman Catholic version of it) purports to be. I regret to say that you would not recognise the Church today. But perhaps you would. I do not imagine that corruption is a recent phenomenon.

I have wondered how, as a monk living an austere existence, you came to be a painter, but I have read that your older brother taught you the skills and a member of the Medici family provided your materials. Did it give you the freedom, I wonder, to paint as you wished, or did patronage produce constrictions? Either way, you were at least free of the need to write funding applications, or to worry about whether your practice was commercial. (We all have our crosses to bear.)

My own early education was firmly lodged within the Christian tradition. One month after my fourth birthday, I was sent to a Melbourne school run by Anglican nuns (for the purposes of this letter, I must assume that you know of Protestantism, the Oxford Movement and in fact the existence of Australia) and there I remained until the age of seventeen, practising the rituals of the Church of England and learning the basic precepts of Christianity as described in the King James Bible, an account that could at least be regarded as poetic, unlike the biblical translation currently in use which has been presented, rather belatedly one feels, as Good News.

It was disappointing to be forced gradually to conclude that the teachings of the dear sisters were a complete anachronism, more suited to your time than mine. In an effort to save the baby while ditching the bathwater, I explored many manifestations of belief, starting with evangelism at age twelve, retreating to a flirtation with Judaism in my late school years and then, when I began my adult life, exploring the various faiths (and their offshoots) practised throughout Asia (it was the 1960s, after all).

It took a long time for me to realise that Man (and I'm happy to refer to humanity in its solely masculine form in this case, since Christianity's ruling faction was entirely male) had in fact made God in his own image, not the other way around. (I must ask you to forgive my apostasy. It couldn't be helped.)

While reaching this conclusion, I was studying Fine Art in the unlikely setting of Darwin, in a community college that was in the process of becoming accredited as a university. Despite the location of the art school, only European art was on the agenda. The irony of studying European art in a place burgeoning with stunning Aboriginal work was apparent. The art school was – I don't mind saying it – an inadequate one. However, no learning is, in the end, a waste of time.

Art History, as presented by the art teacher from the local high school when no one more suitable could be found, was approached chronologically. It began in Lascaux and by the end of the first year we had reached Picasso. So it was early in first term that I came upon your paintings while researching the art of the Early Renaissance.

Somehow, your paintings managed to bring into that chaotic and superheated atmosphere a breath of incense-laden air cooled by European stonework; and it brought to me a personal renaissance. It enabled me to reconnect fragmented sections of my life.

Sitting under the fluorescent lights of Darwin's public library, I was somehow able to recapture the experience of being in a kindergarten class in a pleasant Victorian room singing 'Around the throne of God a band of glorious angels always stand – Bright things they see, sweet harps they hold, and on their heads are crowns of gold.'

The imagery arising from your unquestioning belief matched the remembered innocence of my childhood and, in doing so, restored to me something important that I had somewhere misplaced – a wholeheartedness, perhaps – a happiness uncompromised by later learning. The metaphorical baby had been plucked from the drain undamaged.

Of course, I value knowledge very highly; but a radical shift in thinking does sometimes cause a dislocation, a feeling that one is wandering without a map. Your paintings reminded me of the point from which I had set out on my journey, and thus enabled me to understand the route I had taken and to make sense of where I had ended up. This was a great gift, and I wholeheartedly thank you for it.

The community of Darwin in those days (the late 1980s) was truly international, a salmagundi of south-east Asians looking for a safer life, Italians who had drifted north from Western Australia after the post-war migration, Portuguese who had come via Timor, Chinese descendants of the gold rush, Greeks (I don't know when they had arrived but among other things they owned the only decent grocery in town), Aboriginal people who had been there all along, and people like myself who had come from the southern states for strange and unexpected reasons and hadn't yet decided to leave. It was a great place in which to look for and, eventually, to find oneself.

There is no apparent connection between your fifteenth century paintings and the Aboriginal art that I was only just discovering at that time, and yet both were a source of inspiration to me. It was to do, I think, with sincerity. Both were expressions of belief. Both were intended to focus understanding and to preserve and promote knowledge of those beliefs within their communities. The particulars of belief, I hasten to add, are less important than the spirit in which the art was created.

For me, the authenticity, the personal truth with which one approaches the making of art, defines the art. This gave me (eventually) a way forward in my own work. I share neither your beliefs nor those of the Aboriginal peoples and yet, within myself, in the secular world that I inhabit, I recognise a feeling that all of us share, and that I believe must be maintained in order for our worlds to prosper. For me, it is a kind of wordless, amorphous understanding. But this feeling is what drives my painting.

You were truly a master of painting, Fra Angelico, and your devotion lights your work. I am not the only one who has noticed: a recent Pope, I do not remember which one, made you officially 'Beato Angelico', 'Blessed Angelic One', no longer simply 'Fra'. I hope though that you will not mind if I still address you as a brother; perhaps a brother in art.

And if by chance you do happen to be with the Holy Ones, please remember me to them. Tell them I'm doing fine.

With all sincerity,
Faridah

To Margaret Preston

8 April 2022

Dear Margaret

The National Gallery is currently showing an exhibition entitled Know My Name, a survey of the work of 150 Australian women artists, designed to bring them at last to notice. It's a delight to see so many of my favourite artists banded together. Your 1930 self-portrait was chosen for inclusion.

Your name, of course, has never been forgotten. Your prints of Australian flora were among the first works of art that really appealed to my school friends and myself in the late 1960s, not long after your death, and they are still well known and loved. However, I owe you an apology, which is what has prompted me to write.

Studying art in Darwin in the 1980s, I was asked for an essay on an Australian artist. I chose you. Then in my thirties and raising five children on my own, I had little enthusiasm for Drysdale's skinny cricketers and Nolan's Ned Kellys. I might as easily have chosen Joy Hester, but I didn't want to get into the Heide scene. Vases of banksias were easier.

When I looked more closely, I discovered that you had at one time included Aboriginal motifs in your work. Before arriving in Darwin two years earlier, I had had no real contact with Aboriginal culture. This was typical of the times. In the Northern

Territory, however, one soon became aware of the complexities of what our British ancestors had perpetrated.

I learnt that land rights were a hot topic: Gough Whitlam had handed back Uluru in 1985, but the Mabo decision acknowledging native title was not made until 1992. I had no awareness, even then, of the tragedy of the stolen generation; Kevin Rudd's formal apology was still twenty years away. However, Aboriginal art had been consistently reproduced on tourist souvenirs for decades and by 1988 the practice had earnt widespread disapproval. Consequently, (and without wishing to bracket your paintings with ash trays and tea towels) when I came across these Aboriginal motifs I saw it as appropriation.

I look back with regret at the very critical essay I wrote. It was only years later that I came to understand how adventurous you were to attempt a cultural amalgam in your art. A little naivety about appropriation can surely be forgiven.

All this came back to mind recently when I was invited to take part in an exhibition themed around Still Life. Of course I thought of you and your Sturt peas and gum blossoms, and of all the women artists of your generation whose subject matter was restricted largely to vases of flowers. I don't know what I will produce for the exhibition but cut flowers will not appear without a tinge of irony. I will, however, think of you and of your determination to produce something that moved beyond the accepted, the merely domestic.

In my research for that essay, I remember, I also came across your print The Expulsion, in which an Indigenous Adam and Eve are being ushered out of the garden by a berobed white angel. I realised that it was your take on colonisation and perhaps specifically the role played by Christian missionaries, but at the time I thought it sentimental and simplistic. However, the journey of a thousand miles begins with one step and I see now that you had made that first step towards acknowledgement and equal rights, way ahead of most Australians. The Expulsion is dated 1952; Aboriginal people were not even counted in the census until 1971. It is only possible to take the first step from wherever you happen to be, and the White Australia Policy is where we were in 1952. In my studies, I was, in some ways, just coming into consciousness of the world around me. I lacked perspective. I'm sorry that I made you the butt of my newfound political consciousness.

I recently saw your Implement Blue at QAGOMA and thought it was terrific. And I have retained my fondness for your linocuts of Australian native plants. I'm grateful to have lived in a time that allows women more freedom of expression. I'm sorry that you're not around to share it – I'm sure you would have made the most of it.

With fond regards,
Faridah

To Mark Rothko

26 November 2021

Dear Mr Rothko – Mark.

As I'm in my seventies and you are actually dead, might we dispense with the social niceties?

It's about a painting of mine. Where shall I begin? Perhaps in the middle, and work towards the edge; that seems to be the way.

In the middle is a body of water, a lake or a lagoon perhaps. A distant shore is visible. In the foreground, the sand darkens in places where topsoil has washed down from the banks. There are no plants. There was sedge, but it had to go. Too literal and, reflected in a puddle, too pictorial, too romantic. But that was in the beginning.

In the beginning was the word, because the word tells you exactly, or tries to. Unlike the painting, which is much more open to interpretation. Or should be. That was the mistake I made.

It was because I loved the place so much. Big Lagoon, it is called. (The word, you see.) A great tray of water, silver the first time I saw it, grey the second (although I always think of it as blue for some reason), with an actual seven swans aswimming on it. Imagine! Sedge standing straight as wire until old age forced it to bend gracefully to the ground, as I hope eventually to do. Unlike yourself; I hope I won't need to take the shortcut to the abyss.

The first time, a swan cried out. I had never heard the trumpeting voice of a swan before. The second time, a rainbow appeared in full arc and a plover shrieked. Who could not be seduced by all this and try to replicate the experience in some way? But the painting just didn't work.

Here's a word: dud. It was a dud.

A palette knife is a handy thing even when you don't use a palette. Good for scraping back. So I did. And now I'm back in the middle, the middle of the painting, the middle of the story. The water remains untouched, as does the sky that colours it, but the shores have been smoothed to their sandy foundation, stripped of anything green. Such an awkward colour, green. I can't remember you ever using it much yourself.

The painting is nearing completion now. All that remains is ascending horizontal bands of hazy colour: sand – water – sand – sky. And that's why I think of you. It looks nothing now like Big Lagoon, but it feels like it. May I quote you? 'A painting is not a picture of an experience, but is the experience.' Nice one, Mark.

The Tate Modern has a room full of your works, with benches in the middle. I know you liked to keep control of your hanging spaces but I don't think you would disapprove. Being there, sitting on the bench, is the only time I can remember feeling that I was caught indefinitely in the middle of a liminal experience, held in suspension, with no idea of the zone I was about to enter.

Your paintings are powerful things. If I read Clement Greenberg correctly (and I may not have done – I was young at the time), he seemed to think that they were all about paint. They're not, of course. By your own account, they're all about emotion; violent emotion at that, and fear. An amazing thing you said: 'I fear the black will swallow the red.' And I gather it did in the end.

There isn't any red in my painting of Big Lagoon, or black, although I have allowed myself a line of indigo to stand for bird call. My own hope, if I may resort to an analogy, is that the blue will swallow the beige, and you can take that any way you like. End of painting, end of story.

I love your paintings, Mark. Thank you. Beyond that, I have no words.

Faridah

To Nyapanyapa Yunupingu

5 March, 2022

Dear Mrs N. Yunupingu

As is the custom among your people, I will not use your name for fear of keeping your spirit bound to place and time. I thought of writing to your sister Gulumbu, whose work also means a great deal to me, but I feel as if she is indeed completely gone from this earth. She was recorded once as saying that the stars are the spirits of Yolngu people when they are not in corporeal form and, looking at her work, it would make perfect sense that now she is there among them, far away. You, however, have only left this earthly life a short time ago.

Last week, I saw your work, and that of your sisters Gulumbu and Barrupu and others, at the NGV. I am lucky enough to own screen prints and etchings by each of you, so I knew what to expect. The exhibition was wonderful, and I was so glad to see you acknowledged in that way. I could have stayed all day and gone to sleep there that night under Gulumbu's painted stars. Among your paintings, I felt so at home.

The 'Bark Ladies' paintings were all from Yirrkala, close to where my son used to live. I visited the art centre many times and you were pointed out to me, sitting on the concrete outside the front door. You were working in isolation, and I was told that the other ladies were in the habit of throwing stones at you. They called your paintings 'rubbish paintings' because they bore no resemblance to the symbols and motifs that had been passed down to you. But the painting I saw you working on was not rubbish. For me, it had a spontaneity that gave it huge energy, the energy of life itself, without the need for any material reference other than the ochres and bark of its construction.

Your story is well-recorded – your terrible encounter with the buffalo, your low status because you were a widow and childless. No one would envy the life you led. And yet, this beautiful work has come out of you, flowing like water, like air, as if all social considerations had been abandoned and you were still a part of the natural world. The rest of us have to arrange ourselves, present ourselves, to match the requirements of the society in which we live. Perhaps your rejection freed you from cultural constraints, allowing you to assume a more natural, unmediated state that the rest of us can only imagine.

I salute you, Mrs N. Yunupingu. Thank you for the great paintings.

As you return to the earth, the sea, the stars from which you came, I bid you a very respectful farewell.

Faridah

To John Olsen

11 July 2023

Dear John,

You've gone. And now I can address you with honesty. The truth is, John, that I've never really liked your paintings. I know this puts me in the minority. Since your death, you've been lauded as perhaps Australia's greatest landscape painter.

I first came across one of your paintings years ago at the Northern Territory Museum and Art Gallery. Perhaps it wasn't the best one you ever did, but it featured the little sunlike, anemone-like, somehow fist-like motifs that characterised much of your work, in muddy colours. I was living in the Territory then, learning about the land itself and its original inhabitants. Compared to the Indigenous paintings of the land, which were so affecting, I'm afraid yours seemed like random wanderings and daubs.

A year or two ago, I went to your retrospective at the NGV and, sadly, I remained unimpressed. I can't seem to track down the reference, but somewhere I saw your work described as a milestone in the development of Australian landscape painting. Maybe the absence of a horizon line is enough to suggest a move in the direction of an Indigenous interpretation of country, some sort of cultural morphing. Is that what is meant by 'Australian'? Isn't it interesting that whoever made the claim used the word 'milestone', a marker for a system of measurement invented by the Romans. 'Landmark', within the context, might have been a more appropriate choice.

We descendants of colonists have so little understanding of the land in which we live. We're not properly integrated into it in the way that Indigenous people are. Paintings from places like Yirrkala and Warmun are radically different in style from one another, but always the work is balanced and harmonious, underpinned by an identification with place, other life forms, story. Your abstractions seem gestural rather than meaningful, at best a personal iconography. Nothing wrong with that, but there's still the matter of the image as a whole. Without wishing to condemn your entire oeuvre, which varies widely of course, but thinking of the abstract landscapes for which you are famous – I suppose I just don't like mess.

I look at your documented history and it seems that you were focused on your painting at the expense of many other things. It looks to me as if members of your family suffered, yet somehow that appears to be justified in terms of you doing what your art required. I wonder how, at the end of your life, you felt about that? You have expressed a certain amount of regret, but that doesn't really count if you knew damn well what you were doing at the time. I'm afraid the notion of 'genius' ploughing its way through life seems to me to be a rationalisation born of egotism.

Your example, of course, raises the question of which work finds its way into the public collections and, ultimately, which is remembered and which is not. As an artist myself, should I be out there chatting to the right people, developing a public persona perhaps? Being noticed? I think you must have enjoyed that part of it, but I'm afraid it's not in my nature. I would love it if my paintings were seen to have some lasting worth, but it seems unlikely. Should I buy a beret?

I realise it's presumptuous of me to pass judgement like this. What do I know? One's response to art is always personal and subjective, coloured by experience. What matters most to me is that I do my work with authenticity. With a good heart. I started my career quite late; I was busy having a family and my family would always outweigh anything else.

But surely, John, one of the most important and joyful aspects of art is its variety. Piece by piece it shows our individuality, our attitude, our opinion, our character: our response to life as we know it. It tells who we were and what we thought right then. Collectively, it tells the story of a time and place, of a society, of a culture. Art is our existential statement. In that, I know we agree. And the response of each one of us when we look at a piece of art is just as individual. If we were all the same, where would be the fun?

I raise a parting glass to you.

And – cheers, John – here's to art!
Faridah

About the Author

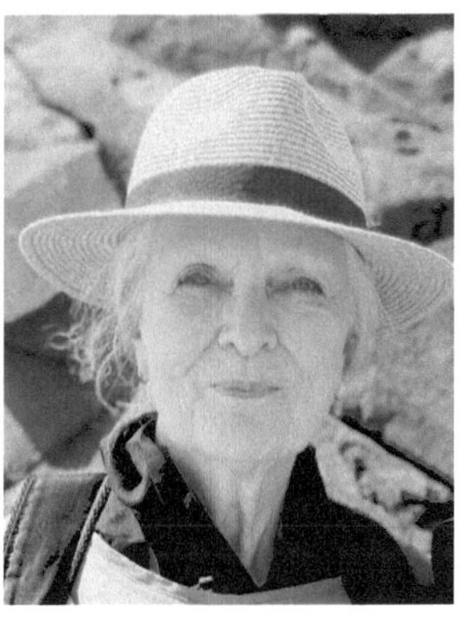

Faridah Cameron is a painter whose art has evolved from her experiences in many different cultural environments in Australia and overseas. In 1991, after completing her BA (Fine Art) in the Northern Territory, she co-founded visual theatre company Neil Cameron Productions as co-director and principal artist. She has taught in schools, universities and communities Australia-wide. In 2004 she gained a Master of Fine Art degree from Queensland University of Technology and moved to Hobart where she altered the focus of her work to full time studio practice. Her work is held in private and public collections including Artbank, the Tasmanian Arts and Heritage Office and the Holmes à Court Collection. She has been short-listed and highly commended in art prizes here and overseas. She is mother, grandmother and great-grandmother to an ever expanding family and long ago lost the ability to distinguish between art and life.

www.ingramcontent.com/pod-product-compliance
Ingram Content Group UK Ltd.
Pitfield, Milton Keynes, MK11 3LW, UK
UKHW040028200726
13854UKWH00001B/418